DOING WORK WITH SIMPLE MACHINES

WORKING WITH
LEVERS

RONALD MACHUT

PowerKiDS
press.
New York

Published in 2020 by The Rosen Publishing Group, Inc.
29 East 21st Street, New York, NY 10010

Copyright 2011; revised edition 2020

Editor: Elizabeth Krajnik
Book Design: Reann Nye

Photo Credits: Cover andresr/Getty Images; p. 7 Jamroen Jaiman/Shutterstock.com; p. 10 Zynatis/Shutterstock.com; p. 11 Karyna Che/Shutterstock.com; p. 12 RossHelen/Shutterstock.com; p. 13 Angel Simon/Shutterstock.com; p. 15 cirkoglu/Shutterstock.com; p. 17 NagyDodo/Shutterstock.com; p. 18 QiuJu Song/Shutterstock.com; p. 19 Pavlo Lys/Shutterstock.com; p. 20 joseph rahi/Shutterstock.com; p. 21 Ramón Espelt Photography/Moment Open/Getty Images; p. 22 Jupiterimages/Stockbyte/Getty Images.

Library of Congress Cataloging-in-Publication Data

Names: Machut, Ronald, author.
Title: Working with levers / Ronald Machut.
Description: New York : PowerKids Press, [2020] | Series: Doing work with
    simple machines | Includes index.
Identifiers: LCCN 2018027006| ISBN 9781538343616 (library bound) | ISBN
    9781538345283 (pbk.) | ISBN 9781538345290 (6 pack)
Subjects: LCSH: Levers–Juvenile literature.
Classification: LCC TJ147 .M2255 2019 | DDC 621.8–dc23
LC record available at https://lccn.loc.gov/2018027006

Manufactured in the United States of America

CPSIA Compliance Information: Batch #CSPK19: For Further Information contact Rosen Publishing, New York, New York at 1-800-237-9932

CONTENTS

LEARNING ABOUT LEVERS

You've probably used a lever today without even knowing it. Did you play on a seesaw at recess? Did you help your mom in the yard by pushing a wheelbarrow? Have you ever held a fishing pole or swung a baseball bat? If you have, you've used a lever! Each of these objects uses **leverage** to raise or move a load.

Levers are simple machines. A simple machine is a **device** with few or no moving parts. These devices are used to modify, or change, motion and force to do work. The lever is one of six simple machines.

MECHANICAL MARVELS

Some devices are made up of more than one simple machine. They're called **compound** machines. A wheelbarrow is a compound machine made up of a wheel, **axle**, and lever.

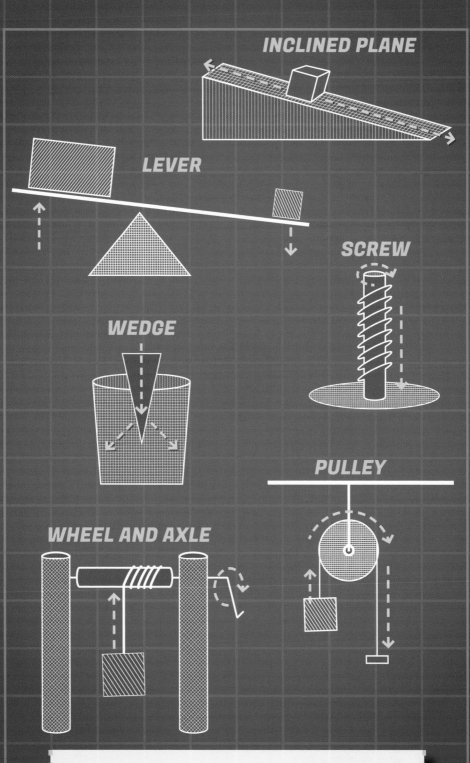

INCLINED PLANE

LEVER

SCREW

WEDGE

PULLEY

WHEEL AND AXLE

The other simple machines are the pulley, the inclined plane, the wedge, the wheel and axle, and the screw.

5

THE PARTS OF A LEVER

A lever is made up of two parts: a **plank** and a fixed point called a fulcrum around which the plank pivots, or turns. People often use levers to help lift or move heavy loads. Levers can also be used to force one object away from another.

All simple machines provide mechanical advantage, which is the machine's ability to multiply the mechanical force applied to the load. To lift a load, the force applied to the load must be greater than the **resistance** of the load. A lever helps increase that mechanical force.

Levers are very **efficient** machines. This means that a lever doesn't waste the force you apply to it.

CLASSES OF LEVERS

Levers are grouped into three classes, or kinds, based on the position of the fulcrum, the load, and the force used. The three classes are first class, second class, and third class.

In first-class levers, the fulcrum is between the force and the load. A common example of a first-class lever is a seesaw. In second-class levers, the load is between the force and the fulcrum. A common example of a second-class lever is a wheelbarrow. In third-class levers, the force is between the load and the fulcrum. A common example of a third-class lever is a stapler.

Using these pictures, think about the levers you see every day. Can you find examples of levers in your classroom?

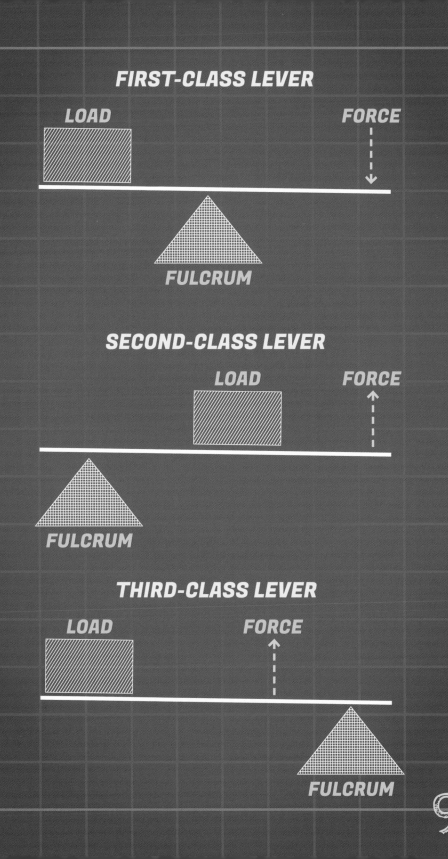

THE FIRST-CLASS LEVER

In first-class levers, the fulcrum sits between the force and the load. Downward force is applied at one end of the plank. The fulcrum changes the direction of the force, which drives the other end of the plank upward.

MECHANICAL MARVELS

It's easier to lift a load if the distance between the load and the fulcrum is shorter than the distance between the fulcrum and where the force is applied.

Two first-class levers joined at the fulcrum are called double first-class levers. Pliers, scissors, and **chopsticks** are examples of double first-class levers.

One example of a first-class lever is a seesaw. On a seesaw, the lever is the long plank on which children sit. The fulcrum is the bar at the middle of the plank on which the plank rests. The children sitting on either end of the plank take turns acting as the force and the load.

THE SECOND-CLASS LEVER

In second-class levers, the load sits between the force and the fulcrum. The force and the load move in the same direction. Force is applied upward at one end of the plank to lift the load.

Two second-class levers joined at the fulcrum are called double second-class levers. A nutcracker is an example of a double second-class lever.

One example of a second-class lever is a wheelbarrow. The plank goes from the handles down to a wheel at the other end. The load sits in the middle, and the middle of the wheel is the fulcrum. Upward force is applied to the handles to lift the load.

THE THIRD-CLASS LEVER

In third-class levers, the load sits at one end of the plank with the fulcrum at the opposite end. Force is applied somewhere between the load and the fulcrum. If force is applied closer to the load, the load is easier to move. In third-class levers, the force and the load move in the same direction

Third-class levers are different from other levers because it takes more effort for a third-class lever to move a load. However, once force is applied, third-class levers can make a load move quickly.

Your arm is an example of a third-class lever. Whatever is in your hand is the load, your elbow is the fulcrum, and your upper arm **muscle** acts as the force.

ANCIENT LEVERS

Farmers in ancient Mesopotamia—which is now much of modern-day Iraq and parts of Kuwait, eastern Syria, and southeastern Turkey—may have been some of the first people to use levers. Starting around 3000 BC, these farmers used a machine called a shadoof to help them water their fields. A shadoof is made up of a tall, wishbone-shaped pole that acts as a fulcrum, with another long pole laid across it as the plank. A bucket hangs from the long end of the pole and a weight is attached to the short end.

MECHANICAL MARVELS

In the third century BC, Archimedes, a Greek **mathematician**, became perhaps the first person to explain the mechanical advantage of the lever.

A shadoof is a first-class lever. Some people in Asia and Africa still use these levers for lifting water today.

MODERN LEVERS

One of the most common places we see levers being used today is in heavy **industry**. One example of an industrial lever is the oil pump jack. This machine is used to lift oil out of wells dug deep into the ground.

PUMP JACK

Tower cranes, which are a type of first-class lever, are used at many construction sites to lift building **materials** and large tools. The long arm carries the load and the short arm balances the load with heavy weights.

Pump jacks are first-class levers. A motor creates the force, which drives a long arm up and down. This beam rests on a tall, A-shaped frame, which acts as the fulcrum. There's a weight at one end of the beam. At the other end of the beam hangs a long **cable** that raises and lowers a metal rod deep underground to draw out the oil.

LEVERS FOR EVERYDAY USE

We use levers every day. However, we might not always realize it. Scissors are an example of a double first-class lever you might use every day. You apply force to the levers by pulling the scissors' handles together. The fulcrum changes the direction of the force you apply, which brings the blades of the scissors together. The thing you're cutting acts as the load.

Can you find another example of a lever in your school or home? Find the fulcrum, load, and force of the lever. What class of lever do you think it is?

A car jack is an example of a first-class lever. The car is the load, a part inside the jack is the fulcrum, and force is applied to the handle of the jack.

HUMANS HAVE LEVERS!

← - →

The human body is full of levers! There aren't many examples of first-class levers in the human body. An example of a second-class lever in the human body is when someone stands on their tiptoes. The fulcrum is the **joint** where the toes meet the main part of the foot, muscles in the lower leg apply force to the heel bone of the foot, and the load is the human body.

Third-class levers are the most common levers found in the human body. When you swing a baseball bat, your elbow is acting as a fulcrum!

GLOSSARY

axle: A bar on which a wheel or pair of wheels turns.

cable: A strong rope often made of wires.

chopstick: One of two thin sticks used mainly by people in Asian countries to pick up and eat food.

compound: Made up of two or more parts.

device: A tool used for a certain purpose.

efficient: Capable of producing desired results without wasting materials, time, or energy.

industry: A group of businesses that provide a certain product or service.

joint: A point where two bones meet in the body.

leverage: The increase in force gained by using a lever.

material: Something from which something else can be made.

mathematician: A person who is an expert in mathematics.

muscle: A part of the body that produces motion.

plank: Something that supports something else, such as a board.

resistance: An opposing or slowing force.

23

INDEX

WEBSITES

Due to the changing nature of Internet links, PowerKids Press has developed an online list of websites related to the subject of this book. This site is updated regularly. Please use this link to access the list: www.powerkidslinks.com/dwsm/levers